Sleepless Nights

Sleepless Nights
Verses for the Wakeful

Translated by
Thomas Cleary

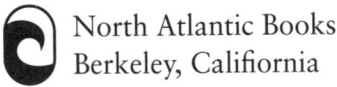

North Atlantic Books
Berkeley, Califiornia

Sleepless Nights: Verses for the Wakeful

Copyright © 1995 by Thomas Cleary. Translated from the original Chinese. No portion of this book, except for brief review, may be reproduced in any form without written permission of the publisher. For information contact North Atlantic Books.

Published by
North Atlantic Books
P.O. Box 12327
Berkeley, CA 94712

Cover and book design by Paula Morrison
Typeset by Catherine Campaign
Printed in the United States of America.

Sleepless Nights: Verses for the Wakeful is sponsored by the Society for the Study of Native Arts and Sciences, a non-profit educational corporation whose goals are to develop an educational and crosscultural perspective linking various scientific, social, and artistic fields; to nurture a holistic view of the arts, sciences, humanities, and healing; and to publish and distribute literature on the relationship of mind, body, and nature.

Library of Congress Cataloging-in-Publication data
Wen-hsiang, Shih, b. 1211.
    Sleepless nights : verses for the wakeful / translated from Chinese by Thomas Cleary.
       p. cm.
ISBN 1-55643-200-3
I. Cleary, Thomas, 1949– . II. Title.
PL2687.W465S58 1995
895.1'142—dc20   94-24048
                                          CIP

1 2 3 4 5 6 7 8 9 / 98 97 96 95 95

Contents

Introduction ... ix

Sleepless Nights: Verses for the Wakeful

A Long Journey ... 3

Song of the Wife of a Soldier at War ... 5

Feelings on a Journey ... 6

Composed in a Dream ... 7

Sleeping Early ... 8

Autumn Scene ... 9

The Sky ... 10

Feeling Spring ... 11

Night Air ... 12

My Mind ... 13

A Lone Traveler ... 14

Gazing at the Moon ... 15

A Mountain Night ... 16

A Solitary Traveler ... 17

Grief ... 18

Thinking of Home ... 19

Elegy of a Soldier's Wife ... 20

Back from a Dream ... 21

Moon on the Border Mountains ... 22

Sleeping in the Clouds ... 23

Enjoyment ... 24

The Third Night's Moon ... 25
A Wandering Wizard ... 26
Feelings on a Journey ... 27
My Sixtieth Year ... 28
Concealing My Tracks ... 29
Roaming Free ... 30
On Awakening from a Dream ... 31
My Mind ... 32
Admonition on Neglecting Mind ... 33
Nursing Sickness ... 34
My Life ... 35
How Long Can a Human Life Go On? ... 36
Roasting My Back ... 37
Lying in the Forest ... 38
Sitting at Dawn ... 40
My Body ... 41
Living in the Mountains ... 42
Tracklessness ... 43
Aging and Illness ... 44
Cinnamon Feelings ... 45
Remote Dwelling (two verses) ... 46
Night Birds Calling ... 47
Song of Silkgrowing Women ... 48
Listening to What an Old Peasant Says ... 49
Racing Horses ... 51

Going Home in a Dream ... 52
Borderland Thoughts ... 53
Night on a Journey (two verses) ... 54
Distant Wandering ... 56
Rainy Night ... 57
Travel Conditions ... 58
Free People ... 59
West Wind ... 60
Sitting in the Clarity the Rest of the Night ... 61
True Pleasure (two verses) ... 62
A Recondite Place ... 63
Staying in the Country ... 64
Farmers ... 65
The Road of the World ... 66
The Span of Human Life ... 67
Warning on Extravagance ... 68
Not Sleeping on a Quiet Night ... 70
An Abandoned Tomb ... 71
Night on a Journey ... 72
Waking from a Dream ... 73
Elegy of a Soldier's Wife ... 74
Ancient Ideas (four verses) ... 75
Song of Natural Happiness ... 79
Feeling the Season ... 80
Night Thoughts ... 81

Walking in the Moonlight on a Hot Night ... 82

Feelings on an Autumn Night ... 83

Feeling Uplift ... 85

Feeling Uplifted on the Road ... 86

Thoughts on a Journey at Year's End ... 87

The Way of the World ... 88

Exhilaration from a Stroll ... 89

Uncramped ... 90

Dawn ... 91

The Sun on the Forest at Dawn
  Melts the Frost on the Leaves,
  Which Drips Like Falling Tears ... 92

Happiness in the Morning ... 93

Sitting Alone at the Edge of the Clouds ... 94

Human Life ... 95

Returning at Night (two verses) ... 96

Introduction

In the early decades of the thirteenth century, Genghis Khan led a confederacy of Mongol tribes out of the steppes of Central Asia to conquer northern China, Turkistan, Transoxania, and Afghanistan, further extending his raids into Persia and eastern Europe. Under the leadership of Genghis' sons and grandsons, the Mongol Empire swallowed the rest of China and established khanates in Turkistan, Persia, and Russia. Apart from those slain in combat, it has been estimated that as many as 30 million people died at the hands of the Mongol hordes.

This book of verses is translated from a huge collection of poetry written by a refugee who lived through this cataclysmic era. The author, whose name was Wen-siang, was born in China in 1210, just before Genghis Khan invaded north China to wrest it from the control of the Jurchen overlords, earlier usurpers. Nearly seventy when Genghis' grandson Kublai overthrew the Southern Sung dynasty, Wen-siang lived for at least another eight years, under the regime of the Mongol conquerors.

Wen-siang's poetry gives voice to the sufferings and the hopes of a people groaning under the weight of history, the conscripts, the peasants, the women, and the refugees. He was an independent Buddhist wayfarer, a pacifist, a feminist, a cosmopolitan rustic; once a political prisoner in his own homeland, he was thereafter a lifelong exile and wanderer. Here translated into English for the first time, his writings mock the folly of tyrants and celebrate the indomitability of life. Full of pathos and beauty, they are among the greatest masterpieces of secular Buddhist poetry.

One of the ironies of literary history is that the individuals known to the world as the greatest poets of China, a land where poetry was regarded as a high art, were in reality disciples and followers of even greater masters, Ch'an poets whose subtle artistry went through and beyond the aesthetic into higher realms of experience hardly susceptible to expression in any other way. Even the most intelligent scholars and writers of China in its golden age could barely follow the wizardry of the Ch'an poets, and this is why, strange to say, the greatest poets and the greatest poetry of China are virtually unknown even in their homeland.

The art of translating Ch'an poetry has never been public knowledge, and is not taught in schools, present or past. Some university scholars today have even expressed the opinion that the symbolic language of Ch'an does not exist. The Ch'an reply would be that this is due to ignorance, confusion, and consequent insensitivity, resulting in an approach to the subject that is much like scratching your shoe to relieve an itching foot.

The selection of the poems presented here in translation for the first time reflects special meanings for the present day, as well as perennial themes for all seasons. To speak of these directly, outside the poetry itself, would be an affront to the delicacy of the issues, the sensitivities of the reader, and, of course, the subtleties of the work itself.

Sleepless Nights

A Long Journey

Far, far, a journey of ten thousand miles;
green, green, the riverbank grasses.
The green green grasses fade and die out,
but the long long journey never ends.

Once Ch'in had destroyed the six states of old,
it drove the people to build the Great Wall.
A great wall stretching thousands of miles
against the warriors of the north.

The sand and water by the wall are so cold
my horse cries sadly when I take it to drink.

The men who built the wall
were exhausted by the toil;
who did not miss his homeland?
They thought of their care for their parents,
and grieved for the families they left alone.

If they died on the site,
their whitened bones
stuck up in the void,
their tallow and blood
fertilized the meadows,
and their souls wandered desolate.
How miserable the builders of the wall;
they raised their shovels with no joyous song.

If protected by humaneness,
a country is naturally secure;

but inhumanity spreads calamity.
The ancestors did not know
wanton violence to make people toil.
The ghosts of the high luminaries
look into their rooms.

The Way of Heaven always dislikes fullness:
The Great Wall was uselessly made so high—
it did not save Ch'in from collapse.
How can that compare to the rulers of
    antiquity
who presided over peace without effort?
Perfect virtue is eternal;
its grandeur cannot be named.

The Great Wall of China was built by the Ch'in dynasty (246–206 B.C.E.), the first imperial dynasty of the Chinese empire, set up by the militarized state of Ch'in after it had destroyed the other major states of ancient feudal China. The short-lived Ch'in dynasty is notorious as a reign of terror, during which countless people died from war, execution, and forced labor on government projects.

Song of the Wife of a Soldier at War

Parted as a newlywed,
like a heroine of yore,
she wonders if it wouldn't be better
had she not married him before.
Her husband's away at the northern wars
for a long time now;
the geese come south, but no word is heard.

The empty bedroom lonely,
the cold nights are long.
The ravaged road goes on and on,
her distant dreams alone.

They say the Taoists
can shrink the earth;
her foolish heart
would seek that magic charm.

Feelings on a Journey

Suffering for lack of resources to live in the
   mountains,
I've become a traveler thousands of miles
   away.
I'm unable to meet my brothers, both parents
   are going gray.

No letters come from my old gardens,
threads of sadness gather day and night.
Then the roots of dry grasses filling the yard
suddenly change again to new green.

Composed in a Dream

>Why grieve at being abandoned?
>Poverty and lowliness are not afflictions.
>Walking by the mountains and rivers
>quite suits the hermit's feelings.
>No cars come to my cottage door;
>green moss fills the long pathway.
>Suddenly hearing the fisherfolk's song,
>I'm moved with the happiness of rivers and lakes.

Sleeping Early

In cold weather I always go to sleep early,
not waiting for the sunlight to withdraw.
I never shut my cottage door,
lest it keep the mountain monkeys out.
Falling leaves strike the window;
at my pillow it seems like raindrops.
Rising, I gaze at the western peaks;
the moon has set, the stars are twinkling.

Autumn Scene

> Autumn's already half gone;
> the wind grips colder each day.
> The ducks come back to visit;
> no trace left of the summer birds.
> At this time the traveler
> is sensitive and thinks of home;
> Even if he can return in dreams,
> the road back is hard to skip over.

The Sky

The sky is filled with ultimate truth;
other and self are both forgotten.
Having a mind like iron,
why care that my hair's grey as frost?
A clear spring follows the valley far,
an old cottage lies deep in the clouds.
This is where I'm at peace,
blissful delight without end.

Feeling Spring

Suddenly sensing spring about to leave,
I amble about taking in the garden grove.
A light breeze scatters remaining red,
a fine rain enriches luxuriant green.
The richness of the green
is like happiness and prosperity,
the scattering of the red
is like dishonor and disgrace:
through them I understand the human world,
how easily all things overturn.
The lowly may rise to the azure clouds,
aristocrats may be slaughtered in crowds.
Calamity and fortune have no fixed borders;
time and again they alternate.
How can we know today's song
will not be tomorrow's lament?
It is written, as a guide for the world,
the successful shouldn't indulge their desires;
be careful as if walking on thin ice,
remember things change as you labor.
If you can learn these principles,
you can follow the footsteps of sages.

Night Air

The night air
has just reached deepest darkness,
but the free man
has already awakened from dreams.
The sound of the north wind snaps,
the lamp in the cottage
is green in the rain.
In the mirror of awareness,
all states of mind are quiet;
forgetting objects,
the body's at rest.
This is beyond the ambitious
who ride on horseback
under cold starlight.

My Mind

My mind is inclined to quiet;
outside of things,
I lodge in the brush.
The sense of the mountains is best
when you reach their depths;
the source of the valley stream, distant,
is naturally purified.
For the rest of my life,
all that's missing is death;
all thoughts and worries
are settled already.
Recluses should leave no tracks;
people stop asking their names.

A Lone Traveler

While everyone else
is so busy striving,
the lone traveler
is at ease by himself.
He's been living outside of convention
for a long time now;
in his pouch there is nothing at all.
When he walks,
he takes a cane for a companion;
when he talks,
he has the rocks for an audience.
If you ask him what his religion is,
when hungry it's a bowl of rice.

Gazing at the Moon

Lighting incense in a quiet room,
I lean against the stone railing,
humming now and then.
Suddenly,
from the green jade river
valley through the mountains
wells forth
a bright silver bowl.
The constellations disappear
in the clear light
shining through me, cold.
Unable to sleep all night,
I gaze on it
twenty-four times.

A Mountain Night

The mountain air
is quiet in the night.
The spring flows
through the shadow
of the stone ravine.
All movements cease
in the emptiness.
A single lamp burns
deep in the cold hall.
The pure white visage
of the crescent moon
clarifies the heart
of a traveler in the open.
Perking up,
he sings an ancient tune;
the wind sways
the old pine woods.

A Solitary Traveler

The chirping insects
in the dark
cry unceasingly;
a solitary traveler
without pleasure
rises in the night.
At a vast distance
the River of Stars
flows due West;
the thousand peaks
are soaked in moonlight
clear as water.

Grief

A million men gallop afar
into the dust of battle;
how many can keep the body
they had when they set out?
Who knows the number of generals
gone to war since ancient times?
All of them have become the spring
in the green green grass of the borders.

Thinking of Home

My home's in a hidden valley
thousands of miles away.
Since I left,
the spring breeze
has come again
forty-nine times.
With no fields to plant,
I don't go back;
my dreams
fall into the scenery
of the mountains and rivers.

Elegy of a Soldier's Wife

Separation hurts the heart
most of all;
three times since he left
she's sent him new clothes.
Even worse,
her spring dreams
have nothing to go on;
in her dreams
he says he'll come back,
and yet
he doesn't return.

Back from a Dream

Back from a dream,
I hear no human voices.
The tall trees
whisper sadly;
it seems there is a breeze.
Arising alone,
I circle the pond
over and over again.
The myriad mountains
lift up the snow
into the light of the moon.

Moon on the Border Mountains

The moon rises from the eastern sea
shining coolly
on the pass to the West.
Men on the march
far from home
dream of return in the moonlight.
And there are dreams in the bedrooms
of traveling the way to the West;
but they're not aware of each other
going along the road.
Deep their longings,
each have weakened and aged.
Foreign pipes play,
so bitterly sad;
what can be done
about this moon
on the border mountains?
Through the night
tears well forth,
tears like golden waves.

Sleeping in the Clouds

A wayfarer hidden in the mountains,
My nature is lazy and crude.
Should the sky overturn
and the earth somersault
I would not mind at all.
Sitting on hay, clothed in hemp,
I live in a mountain fastness.
This one room reed house
is always filled with clouds.
I like the trail of the clouds,
even as they quietly disperse.
Here I pledge
to be a companion of the clouds.
All day long I lie in the clouds,
forgetting about the time.
Returning from dreams
I find the sun shining warm
on my bed of clouds.
Mindless of this and that,
my body is relaxed;
so I go along with ever more
affection for the clouds.
Another year I'll pass away
and the clouds alone will remain;
and the clouds will be sorry
my life was so short.

Enjoyment

Seventy-seven years old,
I'm an old man
hidden in the mountains.
Seeing and hearing exhausted,
I'm as though blind and deaf.
Just dwelling by the mountains and rivers,
I've understood the vanity
of ego and personality.
With an iron mind
and a stone gut,
I rest peacefully in the eventide,
no worse off
than men of authority.
This is really hard to tell
to people of the time;
only the moon
in the high sky alone
clearly understands.

The Third Night's Moon

> The new moon's like a moth eyebrow;
> its distant beauty lasts but a while.
> Though lacking in the shining light,
> the outline of the disc remains.
> On the fifteenth it will be full,
> but how can we know
> from day to day?
> Human life is also like this;
> destitution and success
> are truly hard to predict.

A Wandering Wizard

I dislike the narrowness
of the human world;
I long to be a comrade
of the ancient wizards.
In silence I merge
with the open void,
communing on familiar terms.
Of a morning I often travel
into the purest heaven;
at night I always rest
in the grove and garden.
Already outside
of heaven and earth,
In a whirl I float
lightly aloft.

Feelings on a Journey

The north wind blows
in a desolate wood
noisily rousing
a frigid sound.
The traveler
hearing it in his ears
suffers yet more
from loneliness.
Relatives and friends
nowhere in sight,
strangers' homelands
just beget burdens.
Even foxes, when they die,
lay their heads on their mounds;
but what can be done
on a journey
that lasts throughout a lifetime?

My Sixtieth Year

Already sixty,
so much I've been through.
Wealth and rank
are like floating clouds;
changing and disappearing,
unworthy of regard.
My body's like a pine
on a winter ridge,
standing alone
through the cold.
My mind is like the water
in an ancient well,
thoroughly unruffled
all the way to the depths.
My path is the ancient way,
especially hard
in the present day.
Not easily discerned
are right and wrong;
I sigh and sigh,
sigh and sigh.

Concealing My Tracks

Disdaining the wind and waves
on the rivers and lakes,
I work on deep concealment
in the mountains and valleys.
At my rustic gate
no comings and goings at all;
by myself I view
the morning and evening lights.
When the sun comes out
the mist and fog dissolve;
when the birds fly off
the pine and bamboo are quiet.
In a moment, the sun
declines to the west;
the remaining glow
lingers on the high ridge.
This short life too
is like a stopover;
who in the world
can take note of that?
I would learn from those
who finally left the realm of dust.

Roaming Free

The fun of roaming free
is endless, hard to exhaust.
When tired I sit on a mossy bank,
unaware of the cold sun falling
in my love for the cool
of the breeze in the pines.
Deer descend
to drink of the valley streams;
monkeys arrive
to pick of the mountain fruits.
What I originally valued
were freedom and quietude;
why should I require
that people know of me?

On Awakening from a Dream

A hundred years
are like a long dream;
and while in the dream,
such rushing around!
After awakening we realize
that it had been a dream,
but never has it been known
in the dream's own time.
My life now awakened,
I don't remember the dream time.
There is no end of people
still living in dreams,
in the dim and the darkness,
pitiful, sad indeed.

My Mind

My mind is quiet, chaste,
an endowment from heaven:
To drive it into the cage of the world
would violate its nature.
The people I meet
are not of my kind;
when I want to talk to them
my mouth keeps silent.
Worldly ways have many traps;
every step is full of worry.
Now I've come back to the forest;
lying down at night, I finally rest in peace.
Mountain herbs can be eaten,
and clear springs are good drinking.
Plain cloth clothes fit me best;
I don't want ornate brocade.
This strategy bodes well;
the rest of my life needs no plan.

Admonition on Neglecting Mind

If you nurture the body
but neglect the mind,
you are like a tree full of termites,
having the outward appearance
but empty inside.
Those who know
are fearful of this.
An emaciated body
may be fattened,
but a ravaged mind
cannot be enlivened.
People of yore had a proverb:
Don't let the root go first.

Nursing Sickness

All alone,
without companions,
my house is also empty.
Worn out,
like a dead stump,
I rest to nurse my health.
When morning comes
I open the door;
fallen leaves
fill the mossy pathway—
so swiftly
does time flow by.
How can a vulnerable body
keep pace in a race?
Whistling in the hollows
rises in the tall forest,
helping me
with my drawn-out song.

My Life

My life,
in youth and full bloom,
was spent on the scriptural teachings
with all of my might.
One mind merges myriad objects,
and I got it to work well enough.
In old age,
I'm more easygoing,
following my pleasure
in mountains and waters.
Now it's become a spontaneous game
with no further contest,
winning and losing no more.

How Long Can a Human Life Go On?

How long can a human life last?
A hundred years,
thirty thousand days.
Half is spent in sleep,
and the rest
is hardly assured.
The regalia of social ceremony
are prison articles, all.
Greedy men liking them
clearly have no way out.
Rich socialites
suffer constant stress,
the poor and humble
are always free.
That is why ancient sages
were not constrained
by emperors and kings.

Roasting My Back

The old body
can't take the cold;
the heart just likes
winter sun.
Roasting my back
at the reed door,
the warmth pervades
the flesh and bone.
I think to myself,
in the human world
this pleasure ranks
as number one.
Though they may say
that fur is warm,
the effect can't compare
with this.
No one comes
to my mountain abode;
sitting alone,
I snatch a flea.

Lying in the Forest

Lying in the forest
long years and months
my free heart
is quite alone and clear.
In the quiet
I watch all creation,
and through it
I sense premonitions.
Wood is cut
for its lumber,
tallow is burned
for its light.
Beasts are penned
for cleverness and nimbleness,
birds are caged
for the music of their song.
People who boast
of being knowing thinkers
fetter themselves
hurting spirit and body too.
Even if their achievements are honored,
they may be boiled in the pot.
It has always been thus
now and of old,
but when you remember
it's still a shock.

Worldly exploitation
always brings trouble;
when abandoned by your time,
then you can live to the full.
That is why ancient purists
finally spent their evenings
in a state of serenity.
Luckily I'm an oaf and a dunce;
maybe there's hope
of living the rest of my years.

Sitting at Dawn

Dream broken,
can't get back to sleep;
so I sit in my hut
in the clear early dawn.
On another mountain
the bell has tolled;
on a lone tree
the first singing birds.
All of my limbs
are tuned and limber,
and all of my states
are deeply profound.
Before I've finished writing a letter,
morning light shoots
through the forest branches.
Trusting my nature,
there's nothing outside I seek.
Once quiet,
ten thousand entanglements end;
why work for people in the dust,
a hundred years of useless unrest?

My Body

Man of the east and west,
south and north,
in deepest silence
I live in the crags and ravines.
As I decline with the years,
my sideburns congeal with frost.
Long on a journey,
I've lost the strings of my sleeves.
Why need think of fine meat
when one can fill up again
on plants in the wild.
But I still worry
about having my body;
only when the body dies
is there no trouble at all.
Changing fashions
is not a fine walk;
with every step
I take to the hills.
No dust or dirt
in the realm of my eye,
No right or wrong
in the root of my ear.
I fill my gut
with seeds and fruit,
cover my body
with clothing of cloud and mist.
Why should I think of my poverty?
My wishes are all satisfied.

Living in the Mountains

Since becoming a mountain dweller
I'm at peace and relaxed,
even in dreams and asleep.
I would say the turtle's withdrawal
of head, tail, and four limbs
is one hundred percent more effective
than the rabbit's triple burrows.
Within essence, just one reality;
outside the body, no extra thing.
Physical death will signal the end;
who can I ask to bury the bones?

Tracklessness

Trackless in the crags and peaks
nurturing the real elemental,
at night I eat chrysanthemum flowers
from the bamboo fence;
in the morning I drink drew
from magnolia trees.
The mystic road
is really worth taking;
how is temporal glory
a good enough aspiration?
Throughout all time,
men of repute
just pile up
down in the graves.

Aging and Illness

Aging and illness
are painful, no fun;
I spend all day long
flat on my back.
A little walk in the eastern garden
saddens my heart even more:
The orchids
are totally gone,
the wild grasses
are shooting up.
I have no strength to weed;
heaving a sigh,
I go back
into my lowly shack.

Cinnamon Feelings

The cinnamon's not of a kind
with the peach or with the plum;
only when the dew is cold
do its flowers finally burst open.
Its fragrant branches can be taken
to give an appreciated guest;
but the road is far
and no one can come—
I go back and forth
all day and all night.
When the sadness of separating
is felt through things,
a thousand miles
isn't really apart.

Remote Dwelling

1.
Dwelling remotely in empty freedom
quite suits someone of tranquil nature.
Outside the gate,
no dust of passersby;
fallen leaves
fill the untended path.
As the glow of the sun
droops to the West,
the last reflections linger
on the eastern ridge.
Lighting some incense, I read
Buddhist scripture,
only letting mountain ghosts listen.

2.
Glory doesn't enter my dreams,
and so I take leave
of worry and blame.
Living remotely
these thirty years,
I've made the acquaintance
of all the monkeys and birds.
The bright sun
has long known my heart;
the solitary cloud
never had any tracks.
The ten-foot room
is always silent;
burning incense
I pass the night.

Night Birds Calling

The roof and trees
of the house to the east
are level with the clouds;
every night some birds
come to roost in there.
They sadden to death
the soldier's wife
in the window there;
the government people
have sent the men
to fight up in the north—
for three years
he hasn't come back;
she's been keeping
an empty bedroom.
The birds cry, unceasing,
the woman weeps even more.
The trails of her tears
are like rain
wetting her blouse and skirt.

Song of Silkgrowing Women

For the folk of Wu
the end of the spring
is just when the silkworms
are hungry after three sleeps.
When the houses are poor,
no money for mulberry
to feed to the worms,
nothing can be done
when the starving grubs
cannot make their thread.
Wives and mothers-in-law
talk to each other,
baskets in hand:
"Who knows the pain
in our hearts?"
When mother-in-law was twenty,
she had no wedding dress;
the men in office raising taxes
were roaring like tigers.
When there is no one
on whom to rely,
rely on mother-in-law
and you may yet relax;
but if you have no thread to pay taxes,
it will wreck your home.
Neighbors gone bankrupt
have already drifted away;
the broken fences
and abandoned wells
are sad to a passerby.

Listening to What an Old Peasant Says

A decrepit old man lay unwell
in a curl of a mountain
when elder Shen from the village east
came along, passing by.
First he spoke of hunger this year,
with nothing to stave off the pangs.
Next he told of the complexity
and the cruelty
of the government of the day.
Of the many things he mentioned,
every one hit home,
complete with the roots
and their ramifications;
none of it was false.
For generations the farmers
have worked in the fields;
how could they know anything else?
The more the way of the world changes
the more superficial the customs;
there is no more idea of mutual refinement.
They used all their cash to raise silkworms
without getting any cocoons;
they've worn themselves out
at the plow and the hoe
but the fields are empty of grain.
A thousand open sores,
a hundred holes in their clothes,
truly hard to mend.
Next month men will come
collecting taxes:

Verses for the Wakeful

The poor lack cash
to prepare a reception,
so they sell the goose
and the gander they've raised.
Yesterday the county official
was chasing people down again;
they're just like sparrows
run afoul of a net.
Children and women crying
are not paid any mind;
their hearts are like tangled threads,
with many a loose end.
The neighbor to the west,
the widow woman,
is even more worrisome yet;
she is like a rotting tree,
without a single branch left.
Burnt by their hunger and cold,
they have no sense of life;
mothers and children are drawn
to drown themselves in the river.
Every statement emerged
from a hurting gut;
when he had finished talking,
snivel and tears both flowed.
This is how full of hardship
the life of the people can be.

Racing Horses

Government agents with fast horses
wearing gold threaded clothes
eat the people's tallow and blood,
growing fat as pots.
The men in the fields
work at the plow
but yet they starve to death;
and here you drunkards and gluttons are,
forgetting the famine this year.
Nature looks on all the people
as on a single child;
how can it be unfair as this?
If human groups overwhelm Nature,
still don't be surprised;
if Nature should determine the time,
it would level itself.

Going Home in a Dream

So many years so far from home;
does the life of toil have an end?
Living as a guest, never comfortable,
my sideburns are already grey.
The river wind
sweeping the leaves
blows hard;
the mountain moon
seeping in
starts its decline.
I think of returning,
still haven't got back;
but a clear dream takes me
into the haze and the mist.

Borderland Thoughts

> The youths on distant campaigns
> already have thinning hair.
> Who rewards their achievements
> in a hundred battles?
> No news arrives
> from the empty bedrooms;
> their homelands have become
> realms of dreams for them.
> The moon on the border
> is the go-between of sorrow;
> as they hear the song of foreign pipes,
> the cold sound is even sadder.

Night on a Journey

1.
The autumn nights
seem longest of the year,
the inns more desolate
and colder.
The lamp dim,
a rat comes from its hole;
the weather cold,
bugs huddle in the bed.
My journey has gone on
for months and years on end;
it's easy to sorrow and grieve
over advancing age.
Lucky to have a rustic hearth,
why did I leave my home?

2.
For a separated man
the night is too long;
rising alone,
he sits
on the empty bed.
Bitter the rain
that delays news of home;
autumn clouds
cut off the old village.
The candle, dying,
flames up once more;
the cinnamons, wet,
make no aroma.
If he could succeed
in his hopes to return,
he'd live at peace
in the upper room.

Distant Wandering

Stopping over in the woods,
I find no shack not tumbledown;
traveling by boat,
I avoid the dangerous shores.
Long have I been a traveler,
guest of different lands;
manners ephemeral as they are,
steady relations are hard.
With the grasses growing long,
the sadness of spring goes on;
when the frost creeps in,
dreams at dawn are gone.
When suddenly I hear a stirring
in the corners of the town,
how can my thoughts of returning
ever be pacified?

Rainy Night

My body's like the plants on the water,
even more vulnerable now that I'm old.
I'm off so far away,
who will ever come here?
Dreaming on an empty bed,
I wake in solitude.
The flashing clouds grow violet
with a pair of thunderbolts;
The lone lamp's green in the rain
on a moonless night.
With a sigh of lament
a long song bursts forth;
the sound of the singing
goes into the dark.

Travel Conditions

When the sun goes down,
I take refuge in a village inn,
feeling the misery
of being on the road.
The land is wasted here,
gangs of brigands have shown up;
the citadel is so far away
you cannot hear the bells.
Not many days
are left in the year;
I think of my village,
how far the way there.
Listening to the cock crow
I bundle up in my clothes;
a frosty moon accompanies
my early morning march.

Free People

The universe has free people
whom nothing whatever concerns.
Controlling their thoughts,
they stop all illusions
to find one whole reality.
Having forgotten all about glory,
how could they worry about disgrace?
Since they have no riches at all,
how could they dislike poverty?
Although you may say
the green mountains are fine,
Still know they are objects outside.

West Wind

The west wind's in the falling leaves,
a lone traveler has extra leisure.
The cold waters all
have returned to their holes;
the autumn clouds
haven't left the hills.
A crown bird takes off,
overturning dry grasses;
a raven comes back,
wearing the evening sun.
Who shares this
uncanny enjoyment?
The brushwood gate
just closes itself.

Sitting in the Clarity the Rest of the Night

Before the night is even through,
I rise and sit,
watching fireflies.
The night air clear as water,
the meditating mind
is light as a reed.
The moon outlines
trees on the western ridge;
a bell arouses
homes up above.
There may be those in the dark
who know just how fine
is what I have found.

True Pleasure

1.
Everyone has his pleasure,
but only my pleasure is real.
Once quiet,
myriad thoughts disappear;
not a mote of dust
in the empty house.
Snow cleans the apricots' bones,
mist feeds the bamboo's spirit.
Let bridle and rope
reach far as they may,
they cannot tie up
this untrammeled body.

2.
Another year about to end
in my empty mountain abode:
rivers and clouds,
their trails indistinct;
pines and cedars,
their natures the same.
I arise from my nap
to find the taro roots done;
as the incense fades out,
I finish a scripture.
Who knows that real pleasure
lies within stillness and silence.

A Recondite Place

In this recondite place
there is no bother or clamor.
White clouds always at the gate,
a loud song stirs the canyon.
The realm of this space
is beyond the universe.
I wash my eyes in sweet-flag water,
lighten my body with the root
of the matrimony vine.
In freedom there is supreme delight
that's hard to tell of to worldlings.

Staying in the Country

Staying in a country place,
the days are full of leisure;
leaning on my briar cane,
I go where my legs take me.
On the wild plain
a line of winter ducks;
in hidden villages
the sounds of chickens at noon.
Everywhere are mysterious things;
free people don't linger on feelings.
By the time I get back,
the new moon is up,
shining on me
going into my hut.

Farmers

The farmers have had a good year;
village to village they laugh with joy.
Barley and wheat
spread the fields with yellow,
mulberry and hemp
shade the gates with green.
The nets are catching
catfish and carp;
the pens are full
of chickens and pigs.
At the ancient shrines
under tall trees
drums and flutes play
to welcome the spirits.

The Road of the World

The road of the world
has always been hard;
being remote
stops problems galore.
The Way is won
by means of no desire;
mountains don't mind
if people gaze.
The cold flow is shallow
along the stony bank;
the burning still goes on
far off in the new fields.
I don't mind a lack of liveliness;
the old fellow knows in himself
how to be at peace.

The Span of Human Life

A human life
may last a hundred years,
or thirty thousand days;
but who has ever lived the full
hundred years to date?
Go lightly along with the flow,
and there's some enjoyment in that;
those in continuous toil
are all so pitiful.
Riches and rank only add
burdens outside the body;
the stinking drunk will overturn
the cups in the palms of their hands.
In the end all alike die;
before they're yet dead
they sure cause some laughs.

Warning on Extravagance

To the sagely kings of high antiquity
all that was of value
was their simplicity.
After those times passed away,
the immoderate came to hold sway.
Once the source had been opened,
it went on persistently;
from Ch'in and Han
through Ch'en and Sui
fewer and fewer knew.
They depleted resources
and ravaged the people;
many could not flourish long.
So we know that indulgence
is hated by Nature and Man.
Gold and jade cannot clothe us,
Brocade and embroidery cannot feed us:
the value's in farming and textiles,
while fancy luxury crafts
are parasites of the people.

The Ch'in dynasty (246–206 B.C.E.) unified and expanded China by force; it soon fell to internal rebellion. The Han dynasty (206 B.C.E.–219 C.E.) expanded the empire and constructed an elaborate educational system to rationalize despotism. Later the Han empire contracted and eventually dissolved, through conflict with native peoples of colonized areas as well as corruption and discontent in the homelands. Between Han and Ch'en there were numerous kingdoms and dynasties ruling various parts of the old Han Chinese empire. The Ch'en dynasty

(557–588) was the last of a series of short dynasties set up by warlords in southern China in the fifth and sixth centuries; it was conquered by the Sui dynasty (589–618), which then reunified north and south China with victories over the powerful Turanian and Tungusic peoples domineering the north.

Not Sleeping on a Quiet Night

It's a quiet night,
but I'm not getting to sleep.
The autumn air is specially clear:
frost and dew paint wild growth in the yard,
falling leaves bring down twigs and sticks.
The west wind is noisier yet;
myriad openings hit the same note.
Even the crickets feel sad,
chirping under the floor.
I go out and take in the view;
the blue sky is sewn with stars:
constellations crisscross the sky,
the Pole Star is now at an angle.
A swan in flight comes from the north
far far away, fatigued by the long expedition.
On the way it lost its mate;
how lonely its solitary reflection!
Moved by creatures, I remember someone afar;
I wander back and forth, uneasy in mind.
My heartbreak cannot be told;
Silently, useless anguish fills me.

An Abandoned Tomb

> Wild grasses engulf
> the tumbledown fence;
> I wonder whose tomb this is?
> Cattle and sheep
> graze its high mound,
> foxes and rabbits
> inhabit its empty spaces.
> For a traveler,
> this is a heartbreaking sight;
> where are the children
> and the children's children?
> The sighing autumn wind
> arouses a breeze of sadness,
> a lonely stirring
> in the white willow trees.

Night on a Journey

How still and silent
the travelers' inn.
The bright moon
is at every window and door.
The clear sky is draped
with arrays of stars;
cool dew wets
the bush around the lodge.
With feelings in my chest
I can't fall asleep:
I get up and sit
listening
to the clock tick.
I listen, then stop,
then listen again.
I listen all the way through
the third, fourth,
fifth watch.

Waking from a Dream

How white the frosty moon,
the cold wind ever intenser.
The weather moves tiny insects,
who cry so sadly all night.
How could a wandering child
not think of home at this time?
Thoughts long continued
turned into a dream
gone far away
west of Huang-t'ang.
This dream was tiring indeed,
crossing mountains and valleys
again and again.
Clearly I saw my close friends,
laughing and talking
and calling me back.
Waking up, I find
I'm still on a journey,
homeland distant,
people estranged.
Evanescent life is like a dream;
no need to compare how long it may last.

Elegy of a Soldier's Wife

Lichen spreads over cedar and pine;
they're always found together.
When she tied up her hair to be his bride,
they pledged to grow old together.
Now he's defending the border forts,
the poor wife with no means of coming along.
On the march, he's further away each day;
when, if ever, is he to return?
The only hope is in honorable service
brought to the notice of rulers above;
that he was loyal and always constant,
and the heart of his wife never changed.

Ancient Ideas

1.
It's hard to talk about anything
with the average person today;
the anxious mind is worrying
and troubled constantly.
The ancient Way was to value
the ordinary and easy;
people of today esteem
the mechanically clever.
Liking the old
but living today,
at every meal
I can't eat my fill.
Coming and going
with distaste and doubt,
all I know
is I love the sanderlings.

2.
The rushing water flows toward the east,
the white sun shifting sets in the west.
Through the vast reaches of sky and earth,
how fleeting the poles of the cycle.
They press urgently on the living,
turning their dark hair to white.
The ignorant don't know themselves,
yet are uneasy all the day long.
When desire for gain sinks this body,
the basis is already crippled.
What compares to repairing true nature
to strengthen one's spiritual bones?

3.
How high the old apricot tree,
flowering only in snowtime;
it keeps its own wintry nature,
won't follow the flowers of spring.
A recluse who happened to see it
transplanted it on the shore
of the river through the valley.
Its skinny form has no positive beauty,
its clear fragrance is void of lasciviousness.
It is free and serene like the recluse,
a joy to the recluse heart;
no woodcutters or herders invade
to leave the recluse regret.

4.
The ancient Way of true immortals
is peaceful aloofness, uncontrived;
by this they strengthen the spiritual root
so they might make the longest journey.
The August Emperor of Ch'in
and the Martial Lord of Han
indulged in desires
unmindful of fatigue;
once they had taken command of China,
they wanted to dominate other peoples too.
Their natures were callous, perverse;
neither were the stuff of immortals.
The mirror of heaven is always clear;
how can it be fooled by brazen liars?
Those who don't look into their own hearts
wrongly wish for undeserved gain.
Their hopes end up unfulfilled,
just a laughingstock for posterity.

The First Emperor of Ch'in and the Martial Emperor of Han were imperialists of China who ruled more than 2,000 years ago. Both of them were interested in the possibility that the myth of immortality might be true, and patronized certain forms of Taoism in pursuit of this interest. They were notoriously unsuccessful in their quest, and Taoist writers heap scorn on them for being greedy and possessive in their attitude toward everything, even the Tao.

Song of Natural Happiness

The happiness of birds is in remote forests;
the happiness of fish is in remote ponds.
The happiness of humans is in remote living;
not being remote always brings trouble.
My abode is now remote,
a shack in the grasses and trees.
Happiness comes of itself,
a happiness hard to tell.
If you ask me what my happiness is,
all of it's gotten from nature.
Supreme happiness is nature's to grant;
though we don't know why, it is so.
Happy in the mornings,
happy in the evenings,
this happiness truly complete,
I sing the song
of natural happiness;
let the audience not make noise.

Feeling the Season

The rich earth produces
mulberry and grain
for silk to clothe the people
and cereal to feed them.
In ancient times one ninth was tax,
suiting both public and private:
nowadays is not like of old,
with cruel campaigns
ever multiplying.
Multiplying on and on,
conscription calls come
regardless of season.
Governments are made
to take care of the people;
why instead do they hurt them?
The reason the people are ailing
and no one can give support
is all because of the rulers' demands
that they must try to meet.
Those who weave are always cold,
those who plow are hungry.
No chickens or dogs remain
in the empty villages;
many are the ruined houses
abandoned by refugees.
A greybeard spoke to me,
and what he said was like this.
An old man makes it a song of sadness;
let those who hear it think.

Night Thoughts

Quiet I sit,
no neighbors around,
watching the mountains,
awaiting the moon.
The heat wave's gone by the pond,
a cool breeze starts in the bamboo.
A bat flies at the window,
a lone firefly disappears into the grass.
My mind has an inspiration,
but only a recluse would know.

Walking in the Moonlight on a Hot Night

Dreading the heat,
I sleep no more;
on the empty stairs
I walk the cool moonlight.
The icy disk is flawless,
so bright you can see a hair;
late night clears the liver and lungs
like drinking most pristine snow.
It's like I'm about to change
to a flying mountain immortal
mounted on a phoenix soaring
into the silent void.

Feelings on an Autumn Night

In the autumn mountains
there are no people at night;
the insects are chirping
at the roots of the grasses.
The bright moon shines
on the tall forest;
through the empty window
wind and dew come in.
I'm over forty now,
and gotten nothing done;
at a crossroads
east to west
I'm busy working
all year long.
Both parents are dead
since years ago,
their graves long capped and finished.
My brothers are also impoverished
and cannot afford to give.
Turning my head I think
of the old garden;
clouds of sadness fill
the plains and marshes.
Of all the friends I've known,
hundreds, or a thousand,
not even ten of them
still remain alive.

I notice my withered form;
what can be done
for the rush
of this short scenario?
All night long
I cannot sleep.
Rising and sitting,
I think a thousand thoughts.
Perfected people can forget
even their emotions;
I try to emulate them,
but how can I succeed?
Only by observing
the state where there is no birth
can I remove these teardrops
from the wet sleeves of my robe.

Feeling Uplift

Solitary, I'm always poor,
ever traveling far and wide.
The road of my journey is endless,
aging lessens my strength.
A no-account
abandoned by most,
my face is changed
by wind and frost.
Returning to the travelers' inn
I lean on my staff and sigh;
a single word cannot be cooked,
ten thousand scrolls
are a useless collection;
better to be an old peasant
who eats from the fruits of his labor.
Individual and society
are like ants turning a millstone;
time goes by like a young horse
galloping past a crack in the door.
What have I done in all my life?
My hair has gone white for naught.
Heaven and earth are vast,
hard to rely upon;
but when it comes to immortal wings,
how could they actually fit?
I wish to live remote,
my nest a single branch,
hoping thereby to avoid
the range of bullet shot.

Feeling Uplifted on the Road

Far, far, I walk a long road;
the western sun lights up the wheat.
Turning my head I gaze
on the mountains of the border pass;
I wonder where my homeland lies?
As autumn wind blows in the oak wood,
I cannot restrain my anxious thoughts.
Unable to see those dear to me,
I'm pensive at dusk, but in vain.
Just when I felt pride
in my handsome youth,
I'd suddenly become
an ugly old man.
How long can a life last,
especially if not always guarded?
Those who remain grow less day by day,
while those who have gone are everyday more.
Even if you prosper in glory,
there is no relying on that;
the song of the dew on the grass
is the evanescence of life.

Thoughts on a Journey at Year's End

Endless are the branching byways,
while the years and months slip away.
The north wind wields its frigid force
on the traveler who has no quilt.
This life is pathetic indeed,
half spent in empty sorrow.
Sympathizers all passed away,
there's nowhere to hide in the moonlight.
Separated
from family and friends,
the grief of parting
wells up day and night.

The Way of the World

The way of the world
is full of wind and waves;
the life of the everyday
has a final end.
East and west I drift
in bitterness and pain;
the color of my hair
is not as it was before.
The dancing bird longs
for a safe haven;
the aging horse wishes
for its old stable.
All kinds of beings
may not be the same,
but for each there is
a suitable fit.
Riches and rank
are but happenstance;
why should we keep them
in our craw?

Exhilaration from a Stroll

Sitting still,
my thoughts are cramped;
after a while
I get up again
to take a stroll.
Hiking up my pants,
I cross a shallow current;
following the clouds,
I climb a high hill.
It's now the midsummer month:
magnificent trees luxurious green,
myriad birds sing in concert,
warbling together ceaselessly.
This feels more like
what I inwardly wish;
soon I forget
a hundred worries.
Loosening my belt
I sit on a boulder;
washing my feet
I gaze at the flow
in its endless stream.
Mind empty,
not grasping at all,
body at ease,
now I am free.
Here is a message for those
who seek to nurture life;
this is the point to which
all alike return.

Uncramped

Cramp yourself
and you'll be constrained;
cramp your will
and you'll be inhumane.
Constraint is shame for the self,
inhumanity blocks the Way.
Unshamed in yourself and your will,
near to pure virtue you draw;
follow your nature this way,
and you are one who is free
everywhere in the universe.

Dawn

> The air is clearest at dawn,
> and the view also reaches afar.
> When the sun starts to rise
> on the Eastern Deep,
> it is the high peaks
> that catch the first glow.
> Feeling the harmony,
> I start to sing:
> my voice is not great,
> but no need hitting the notes;
> for this is itself
> the mountains' own tune.

The Sun on the Forest at Dawn Melts the Frost on the Leaves, Which Drips Like Falling Tears

Dry leaves
are especially pitiful:
the cold wind
blows hard on you,
and the sky
rains chilling frost.
I am afraid
you cannot sustain yourselves;
Falling, you return
to the thickets of grass.
Noticing how late it is,
I'm overtaken with sighs.
Morning sun brings signs
of nature's process,
increasing the weeping
for you.

Happiness in the Morning

Happy in the morning,
I open my cottage door;
A clear breeze blowing
comes straight in.
The first sun
lights the leafy trees;
the shadows it casts
are crystal clear.
Serene,
in accord with my heart,
Everything merges
in one harmony.
Gain and loss
are not my concern;
this way is enough
to the end of my days.

Sitting Alone at the Edge of the Clouds

I sit on a boulder
at the edge of the clouds:
far into the distance
the rain falls, mindless.
The waves stilled,
white seagulls alight;
the mountains cold,
yellow leaves deepen.
Where does the hermit live?
The noon bell
brings a clear sound.
As the sun sets,
I find I cannot leave;
the clustered peaks are casting
shadows of the night.

Human Life

Human life,
a hundred years,
is nothing but
a stop on a journey.
Youth and vigor
cannot be kept;
gradually you realize
decline and age encroach.
Even if you succeed
in accomplishing great works,
who can escape
enslavement to form?
With a drawn-out song
I head on back
to boil white stones
in the heart of the mountains.

Returning at Night

1.
The weather unusually clear and mild,
I've hiked a lot in the mountains.
Following the streams
picking aromatic parsley,
piercing the clouds
to get fragrant late tea,
my hidden feelings
relax day by day,
while clamor and dust
go right away.
Riding the moon
I return to my hut,
not even washing
these tired feet.

2.
All my life I've eaten the food
of pure livelihood alone.
With a begging bowl I head
into the human realm.
In the dark of night
I return to my hut;
the moon risen,
the mountains grow quiet:
everywhere I hear
the sound of springs;
with every step I walk
on the shadows of pines.
Washing my feet,
I meditate in peace;
steeped in the clouds,
the stone bench is cold.